The Medieval World

Medieval Towns, Trade, and Travel

Lynne Elliott

Crabtree Publishing Company
www.crabtreebooks.com

Crabtree Publishing Company

www.crabtreebooks.com

PMB 16A, 350 Fifth Avenue
Suite 3308
New York, NY 10118

612 Welland Avenue
St. Catharines
Ontario, Canada
L2M 5V6

73 Lime Walk
Headington
Oxford 0X3 7AD
United Kingdom

Coordinating editor: Ellen Rodger

Project editor: Carrie Gleason

Designer and production coordinator: Rosie Gowsell

Scanning technician: Arlene Arch-Wilson

Art director: Rob MacGregor

Project development, editing, photo editing, and layout:
First Folio Resource Group, Inc.: Tom Dart, Jaimie Nathan,
Debbie Smith

Photo research: Maria DeCambra

Prepress and printing: Worzalla Publishing Company

Consultant: Isabelle Cochelin, University of Toronto

Photographs: Alinari/Art Resource, NY: p. 17 (top); Paul
Almasy/Corbis/magmaphoto.com: p. 31 (right); Archivo
Iconografico, S.A./Corbis/magmaphoto.com: p. 14 (bottom); Art
Archive: p. 21 (top); Art Archive/Biblioteca Augustea Perugia/
Dagli Orti: p. 18 (top right); Art Archive/Biblioteca Estense
Modena/Dagli Orti: p. 10; Art Archive/Biblioteca Queriniana
Brescia/Dagli Orti: p. 15 (bottom); Art Archive/Bibliothèque
Municipale Rouen/Dagli Orti: p. 5 (bottom); Art Archive/
Monastery of the Rabida, Palos, Spain/Dagli Orti: p. 31 (left); Art
Archive/Musée Condé Chantilly/Dagli Orti: p. 11 (top), p. 27
(right); Art Archive/Museo Civico Bologna/Dagli Orti: p. 14
(top); Art Archive/Museo Correr Venice/Dagli Orti: p. 17
(bottom); Art Archive/Museo del Prado Madrid/Dagli Orti: p. 27
(left); Art Archive/Museo di Capodimonte, Naples/Dagli Orti:
cover; Bettmann/Corbis/magmaphoto.com: p. 30 (right);
Bibliothèque de la Faculté de Pharmacie, Paris, France/Archives
Charmet/Bridgeman Art Library: p. 16 (top); Bibliothèque

Municipale, Dijon, France/Giraudon/Bridgeman Art Library:
p. 13 (left); Bibliothèque Municipale, Rouen, France/Bridgeman
Art Library: title page; British Library/Add. 15277 f.15v: p. 11
(bottom); British Library/Add. 24098 f.22v: p. 29; British Library/
Add. 24098 f.25: p. 28; British Library/Add. 27695 f.7v: p. 20
(bottom); British Library/Add. 42130 f.164v: p. 7 (bottom); British
Library/Harley 4375 f.245: p. 26; British Library/Harley 4379 f.64:
p. 8; British Library/Royal 15 D. III f.138v: p. 12 (right); British
Library/Royal 16 G. VI f.74: p. 7 (top); British Library/Royal 20
C. VII f.41v: p. 6 (bottom); British Library/Topham-HIP/The
Image Works: p. 6 (top), p. 9 (right), p. 24; Angelo Hornak/
Corbis/magmaphoto.com: p. 12 (left); Lake County Museum/
Corbis/magmaphoto.com: p. 30 (left); Erich Lessing/Art Resource,
NY: p. 21 (bottom); Mary Evans Picture Library: p. 16 (bottom),
p. 25 (top); Réunion des Musées Nationaux/Art Resource, NY:
p. 18 (bottom left); Scala/Art Resource, NY: p. 15 (top), p. 20 (top);
Adam Woolfitt/Corbis/magmaphoto.com: p. 13 (right)

Illustrations: Jeff Crosby: pp. 22–23; Katherine Kantor: flags, title
page (border), copyright page (bottom); Margaret Amy Reiach:
borders, gold boxes, title page (illuminated letter), copyright page
(top), contents page (all), pp. 4-5 (timeline), p.4 (top), p. 5 (top),
p. 9 (top), p. 19 (all), p. 25 (bottom), p. 32 (all)

Cover: Medieval ships filled with goods from the Middle East
and Asia unloaded their cargo in Italian ports.

Title page: In the Middle Ages, wealthy nobles traveling by
horseback covered up to 30 miles (48 kilometers) a day.

Published by
Crabtree Publishing Company

Cataloging-in-Publication Data
Elliott, Lynne.
 Medieval towns, trade, and travel / Lynne Elliott.
  p. cm. -- (The medieval world)
Includes index.
 ISBN 0-7787-1350-4 (RLB) -- ISBN 0-7787-1382-2 (pbk)
 1. Cities and towns, Medieval--Europe. 2. Social history--
Medieval, 500-1500. 3. Merchants--Europe--History. 4.
Transportation--Europe--History. I. Title. II. Series.
 Medieval world (Crabtree Publishing Company)
 HT131.E544 2004
 307.76'094'0902--dc22
                                     2004000818
                                         LC

Table of Contents

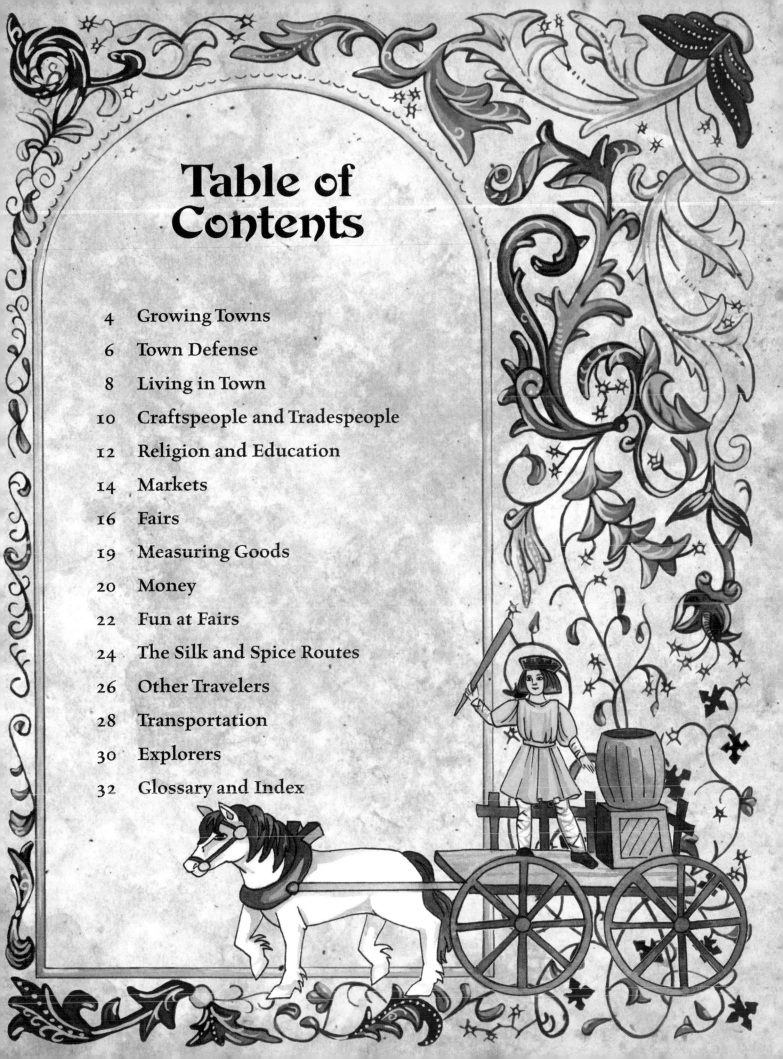

Growing Towns

The Middle Ages, or medieval period, began around 500 A.D. and lasted until about 1500 A.D. in western Europe. During this time, the most important people in society were nobles, such as kings and important lords, who ruled over most of the land.

Nobles gave smaller sections of their land, called manors, to knights who promised to fight for them and advise them about the manors. Knights rented parts of their manors to peasants, who farmed the land, made clothing, and produced other items such as tools.

Anything peasants did not need for themselves or for nobles they sold at markets near castles, churches, rivers, bridges, and **ports**. As the markets grew, craftspeople and tradespeople set up shops nearby. Towns and cities developed from these centers of trade.

▼ *Nobles, who made up only a small percent of the population, ruled over large areas of land that included castles or manor houses, farmland, villages, and towns. Peasants, who made up 90 percent of the population, lived in villages on the manors or were scattered throughout the countryside.*

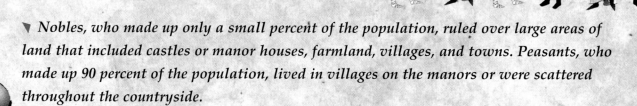

1000s
Viking explorer Leif Eriksson sails to North America

1100s
Venice and Genoa, in Italy, become centers of international trade in Europe

1163
Construction of Notre Dame Cathedral in Paris, France begins

1200s
The compass is introduced to Europe from China; fairs in France become popular

1325
Travels of Moroccan explorer Ibn Battuta begin

900s
Town life grows; the Shrine of St. James at Santiago de Compostela, in Spain, is built

1096
First Crusade to recapture the Holy Land increases trade with the East

1150s
Craft guilds become popular

1170s
Canterbury Cathedral becomes England's most famous pilgrimage site

1271
Italian explorer Marco Polo travels to China

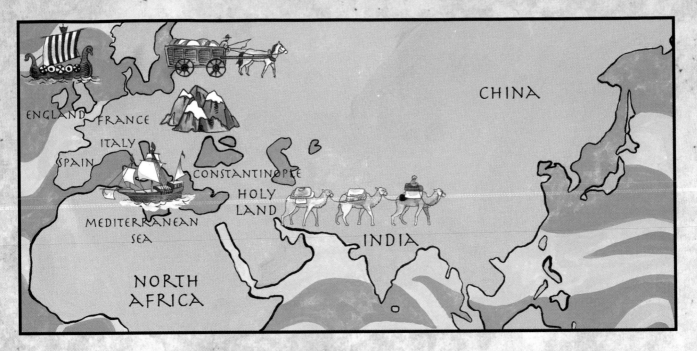

▲ *Most people in the Middle Ages traveled short distances, but some set out on long journeys. Knights, called crusaders, crossed the Mediterranean Sea to protect Christian religious sites in the Holy Land, and explorers traveled to Asia and the Americas in search of new trading routes.*

Medieval Travel

Traveling **merchants** came to markets and fairs in towns and cities to sell goods from far away. They were not the only travelers in the Middle Ages. Students headed to schools and universities, nobles traveled to oversee their lands, and **pilgrims** traveled to places of religious importance.

→ *In the Middle Ages, many towns and trading centers were located along water routes since transportation by water was the least expensive way to move goods and people.*

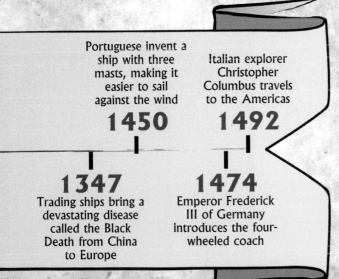

Portuguese invent a ship with three masts, making it easier to sail against the wind
1450

Italian explorer Christopher Columbus travels to the Americas
1492

1347
Trading ships bring a devastating disease called the Black Death from China to Europe

1474
Emperor Frederick III of Germany introduces the four-wheeled coach

Town Defense

Medieval towns were in danger of attack by foreign invaders looking for land and riches, and by neighboring lords and soldiers trying to gain control of the towns from other nobles. Nobles wanted to control towns so they could collect taxes and tolls from the people who lived there and who visited there.

▲ While trying to gain control of towns for their lords, soldiers stole coins, cloth, jewelry, beautiful household items, and animals from the townspeople.

▲ To reach gates protecting entrances into towns, visitors often had to cross drawbridges over moats or rivers. Watchmen locked the gates and raised the drawbridges at night and during attacks.

Stone Walls

Enormous stone walls were built around towns for protection. Town guards defended the walls and, during attacks, the town army, called the garrison, was called in. The garrison was made up of all the men in town. Together, they launched arrows, rocks, hot oil, and burning wood on the attackers from the town's wall.

For extra defense, many medieval towns were built high on hillsides, making them difficult for enemies to attack. Armies that managed to get into the towns often had trouble fighting the townspeople in the narrow, crooked, and often muddy streets.

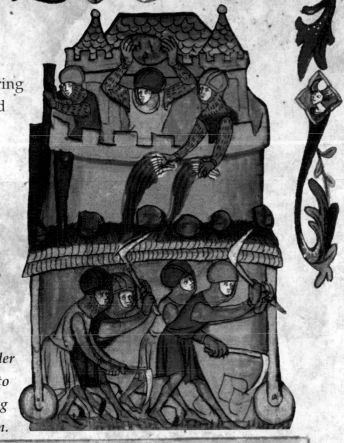

▶ *Attackers who got close to a town's walls hid under a roofed protector, called a tortoise, cat, or rat, to avoid being hit by rocks, spears, and boiling oil that the garrison threw down on them.*

Cities Large and Small

In the Middle Ages, towns and cities in Europe were much smaller than those in other parts of the world. Around 1250, Paris, in France, and Milan, Florence, and Venice, in Italy, were the largest European cities, with populations of about 80,000 people. Cities in the East and **Middle East**, such as Baghdad, in present-day Iraq, Constantinople, in present-day Turkey, and Cairo, in Egypt, had more than 125,000 people. The Aztec capital of Tenochtitlan, where present-day Mexico City stands, had a population of 200,000.

▼ *Medieval Constantinople, now called Istanbul, was a walled city with one side in Europe and the other side in Asia, as it is today. Its location made it an important trading city and stopping place for crusaders on the way to the Middle East.*

Living in Town

Medieval towns contained beautiful stone churches and homes where nobles and wealthy merchants lived. Most townspeople, including craftspeople and tradespeople, lived and worked in smaller buildings made of wood or stone.

Craftspeople and tradespeople usually had workshops on the main floors of their homes. As their businesses or families grew, they built additional stories on their homes. The upper stories were often larger than the lower stories and leaned out over the narrow medieval streets.

Inside Town Homes

The main room of a town home was used as both a living room and dining room. Meals were cooked in kitchens over open fireplaces, and were often made from herbs, fruits, and vegetables that families grew in gardens. Craftspeople and tradespeople also kept pigs and chickens for food. Noble and merchant families grew some food, but bought more expensive meats, cheeses, baked goods, fruits, bread, and wine in town shops.

Townspeople slept in bedrooms beside or above the main room. Beds had straw mattresses, linen sheets, and woolen blankets. Other furnishings included wash basins on tables, a few chairs, chests or cabinets for storage, and poles above the beds for hanging up clothes.

Fleas, bedbugs, flies, rats, and mice were constant pests in medieval homes. People often hung up rags soaked in honey to trap insects. They also set traps to catch rats and mice.

▲ *Buildings in medieval towns were usually very close to one another, sometimes shared walls, and often lacked light and fresh air.*

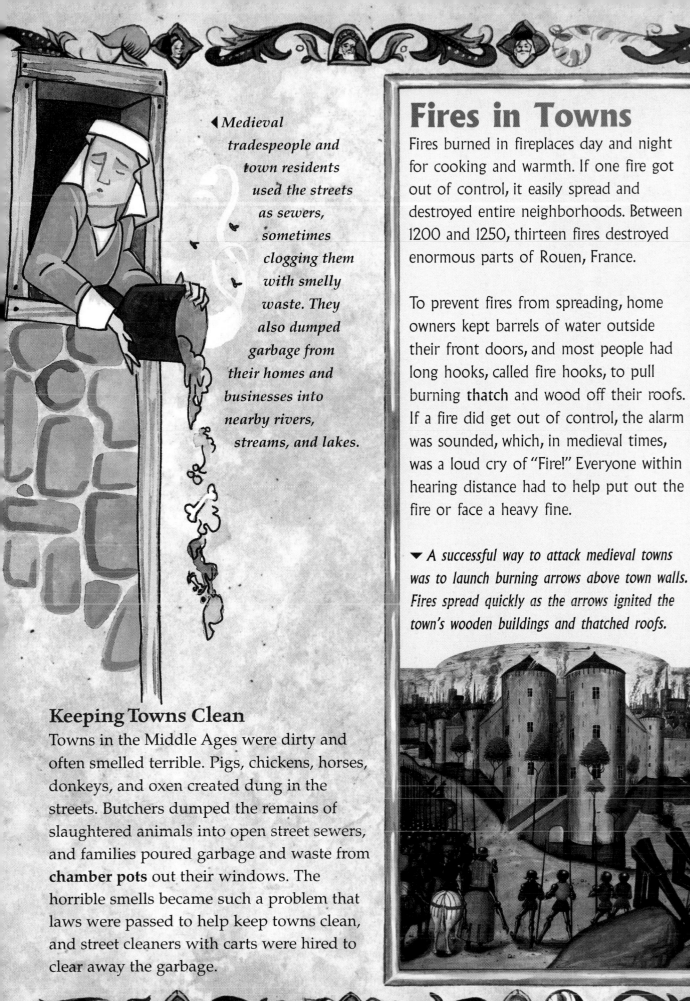

Medieval tradespeople and town residents used the streets as sewers, sometimes clogging them with smelly waste. They also dumped garbage from their homes and businesses into nearby rivers, streams, and lakes.

Keeping Towns Clean

Towns in the Middle Ages were dirty and often smelled terrible. Pigs, chickens, horses, donkeys, and oxen created dung in the streets. Butchers dumped the remains of slaughtered animals into open street sewers, and families poured garbage and waste from **chamber pots** out their windows. The horrible smells became such a problem that laws were passed to help keep towns clean, and street cleaners with carts were hired to clear away the garbage.

Fires in Towns

Fires burned in fireplaces day and night for cooking and warmth. If one fire got out of control, it easily spread and destroyed entire neighborhoods. Between 1200 and 1250, thirteen fires destroyed enormous parts of Rouen, France.

To prevent fires from spreading, home owners kept barrels of water outside their front doors, and most people had long hooks, called fire hooks, to pull burning **thatch** and wood off their roofs. If a fire did get out of control, the alarm was sounded, which, in medieval times, was a loud cry of "Fire!" Everyone within hearing distance had to help put out the fire or face a heavy fine.

▼ *A successful way to attack medieval towns was to launch burning arrows above town walls. Fires spread quickly as the arrows ignited the town's wooden buildings and thatched roofs.*

Craftspeople and Tradespeople

Many people in towns worked as craftspeople or tradespeople. Some trades centered around food. Butchers sold meat, cheesemongers sold cheese, butter, and other dairy products, and spice-grocers sold oils and vinegar, sugar and honey, salt and pepper, and other spices.

Some medieval craftspeople worked in the textile industry. Weavers wove thread into fabric, dyers colored cloth, and tailors sewed clothes. Other craftspeople made items for the home, such as coopers, who made barrels and buckets, and chandlers, who made candles.

Workshops

Craftspeople and tradespeople worked in shops with large windows that opened onto the street. The windows were covered by large shutters that folded down to make shelves on which items made in the workshops were displayed.

Colorful signs hung above the shops advertising items for sale. The signs had pictures instead of words, since many people in the Middle Ages could not read. For example, a winemaker's sign had a bush on it to represent the vines on which grapes grow.

▶ *Glassmakers mixed sand, chemicals such as lime, soda, and salt, and other materials to make glass. They heated the mixture in ovens until it became syrupy, and then placed it on the end of hollow blowpipes. Glassblowers puffed air into the blowpipes while twisting and shaping the glass into goblets, mugs, vases, and bowls.*

Masters

Shop owners were usually experts of their trade, and were known as "masters." Before they became masters, they trained for as long as fourteen years. Then, they presented an expert piece of their work to members of their guild. If the piece was deemed good enough, it was named a "master's piece." The craftsperson was named a master, and he was admitted to the guild.

▼ Embroiderers stitched patterns, such as flowers, birds, and animals, on cloth with needles and thread.

▼ Blacksmiths made and repaired iron objects, such as farm tools, nails, horseshoes, and axes. They heated the iron in forges, or ovens, and hammered it into shape on flat blocks of iron called anvils.

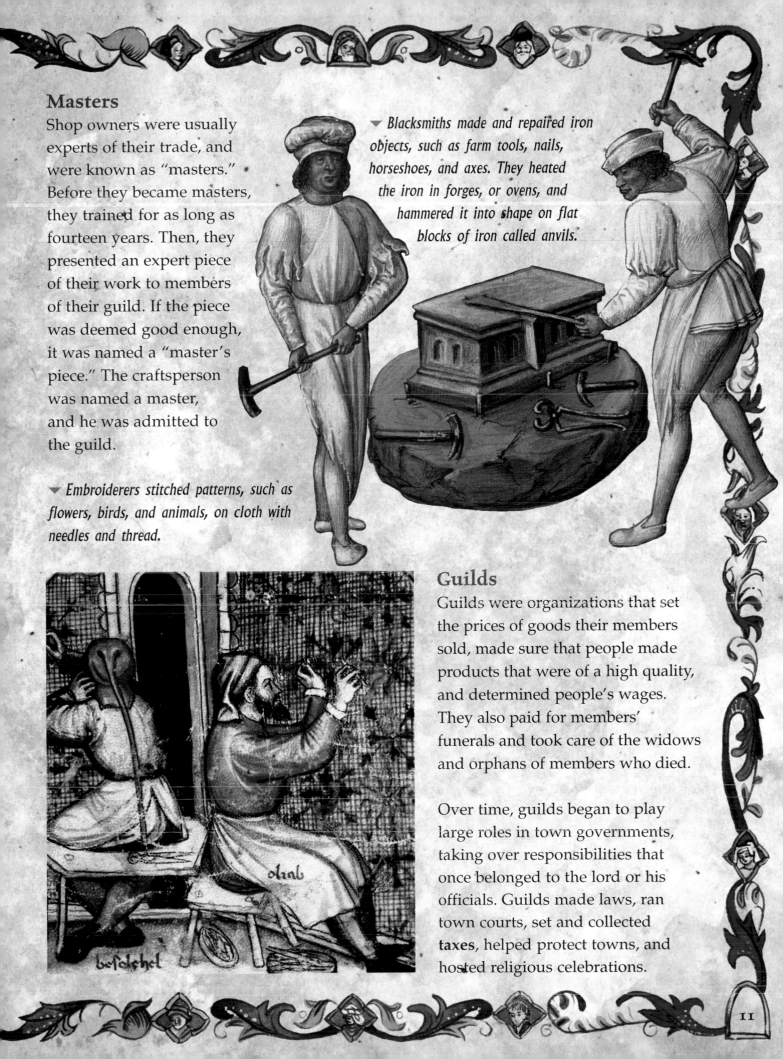

Guilds

Guilds were organizations that set the prices of goods their members sold, made sure that people made products that were of a high quality, and determined people's wages. They also paid for members' funerals and took care of the widows and orphans of members who died.

Over time, guilds began to play large roles in town governments, taking over responsibilities that once belonged to the lord or his officials. Guilds made laws, ran town courts, set and collected **taxes**, helped protect towns, and hosted religious celebrations.

Religion and Education

Towns were often centers of religion and education. The largest public building in town was usually the church. People went there to pray, to visit the shrine of a holy person called a saint, and to ask the priest, who was the religious leader, for advice.

Many community events took place in and around churches. Town officials and guilds held meetings in churches. Pilgrims slept there. During festivals, guild members performed series of plays called mystery plays inside and outside churches. The plays told stories from the Bible and taught people who could not read about religion.

▲ *It sometimes took painters, stonecutters, mortarers, **stained-glass makers**, masons, bell makers, blacksmiths, and metal workers hundreds of years to build a cathedral.*

Cathedrals

In large cities, the main church was called a cathedral. In the cathedral was the cathedra, or seat, of the bishop, who was responsible for all members of the Church in a region. Cathedrals were large, beautiful buildings constructed as gifts to God. They were paid for by members of the church, by wealthy families, and by guilds, who wanted to show off the skills of their city's craftspeople and tradespeople.

◀ *Wells Cathedral, in southwestern England, was named for the nearby springs that were used in religious ceremonies beginning in the 700s.*

Monasteries and Convents

Towns and cities also had monasteries and convents, where people who devoted their lives to God lived. Men called monks lived in monasteries, and women called nuns lived in convents. They spent their days praying, studying, taking care of the poor, sick, and elderly, and offering advice and prayers to the townspeople.

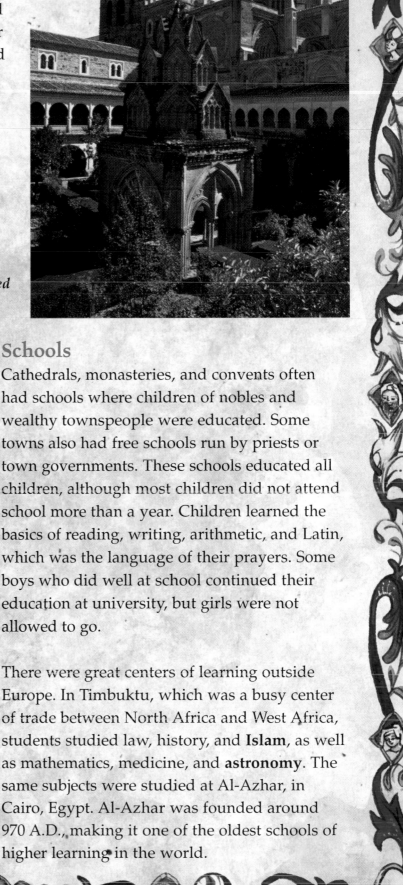

▶ *Construction began on the Monastery of Santa Maria de Guadelupe, in Spain, during the 1300s. Monasteries like this one housed rare collections of books that the monks copied by hand.*

▲ *The first universities in Europe were built in the early 1200s. Students learned by listening to teachers lecture on grammar, arithmetic, astronomy, and music. Good students often went on to study religion, medicine, or law.*

Schools

Cathedrals, monasteries, and convents often had schools where children of nobles and wealthy townspeople were educated. Some towns also had free schools run by priests or town governments. These schools educated all children, although most children did not attend school more than a year. Children learned the basics of reading, writing, arithmetic, and Latin, which was the language of their prayers. Some boys who did well at school continued their education at university, but girls were not allowed to go.

There were great centers of learning outside Europe. In Timbuktu, which was a busy center of trade between North Africa and West Africa, students studied law, history, and **Islam**, as well as mathematics, medicine, and **astronomy**. The same subjects were studied at Al-Azhar, in Cairo, Egypt. Al-Azhar was founded around 970 A.D., making it one of the oldest schools of higher learning in the world.

Markets

Towns were not only centers of education and religion, but of business as well. Towns held markets where shoppers bought all kinds of goods from peasants, craftspeople, and tradespeople. Vendors sold fruit, vegetables, tools, cookware, furniture, live animals, and cloth.

From time to time, merchants at markets sold items that people ordinarily could not get near their homes. For example, some merchants in England traveled to Italy to buy glass and silks, or they went to France to buy mirrors. Over time, some markets became known for trading specific items, such as horse markets, which sold workhorses.

▲ *Weekly markets attracted shoppers from the countryside and from towns.*

▼ *Food peddlers walked around streets and marketplaces and went to people's homes selling items such as bread, freshly baked pies, and a weak alcoholic drink called ale.*

Marketplaces

Markets were usually held once a week in large, open areas of towns. These areas were sometimes located outside important churches or by main streets. Vendors set up stalls in which they hung items for sale, or they covered benches, tables, and carts with their goods. People called peddlers walked around marketplaces selling food and trinkets, such as cups and charms for bracelets.

Organizing Markets

At first, markets were run by local lords. Lords decided at what time markets opened and closed and how vendors should measure their goods. For example, lords determined what weight of hay made up a "bale," and then they charged people to weigh the bale.

Eventually, lords granted guilds permission to run markets and other aspects of town business. In return, the guilds paid the lords a yearly fee.

▲ *On market days, the town's shops, such as the apothecary's shop, which sold medicines, perfumes, and colognes, opened up their windows to the street to attract customers.*

▼ *Lords earned money by renting stalls and tables to vendors at markets, by taking part of the vendors' incomes, and by collecting tolls from people passing through the town gates on their way to the markets.*

15

Fairs

Over time, merchants began to gather at large markets, called fairs, to trade goods from far away. Russian merchants brought furs, Italian merchants brought spices, and Flemish merchants brought cloth.

Fairs were held once a year in towns throughout Europe, usually near important cities, castles, and monasteries. Many fairs took place around major religious festivals, called feast days, when people did not have to work and had time to travel. Some fairs lasted for days while others lasted for weeks.

▼ *Lords welcomed merchants who brought them beautiful, luxurious items. Merchants also provided lords with news about other parts of the world and information about enemies, which they had learned while traveling.*

▲ *Jewelers at fairs sold gems, such as rubies, diamonds, and pearls. The gems were sold alone or were made into beautiful pieces of jewelry.*

Traveling to Fairs

Many merchants endured long, difficult journeys traveling to fairs. They crossed rough seas, swift-moving rivers, and icy mountain paths where snowstorms and avalanches threatened their lives.

Merchants were constantly in danger of being attacked by thieves. To ensure that they, their goods, and their money arrived safely at their destinations, merchants traveled together in groups, called caravans, or they traveled with trained **archers** and armed soldiers. Merchants also asked local lords to grant them letters that guaranteed their safe journey. If they had the protection of local lords, they were left alone by thieves who feared the lords' punishments.

By the time merchants arrived at fairs, they were tired and dirty from their long trips. They visited bathhouses in towns to get clean, then went to inns for a meal and a good night's sleep.

▲ Olive merchants used pack animals, such as donkeys, to carry their goods to and from markets and fairs.

Fairs in Other Cultures

Great fairs were held in other parts of the world during the Middle Ages. About half a million visitors attended the fairs in Kinsai, China's great trading center. They bought and sold meats, fruits, vegetables, spices, and jewelry. Other cities, such as Baghdad, in present-day Iraq, Constantinople, in Turkey, and Damascus, in Syria, had open-air markets, called bazaars. Merchants at the bazaars traded silks and spices from China and India, wool and wheat from Europe, and other goods.

The Opening of Fairs

Fairs began with the merchants registering, or signing up, for stalls or tables in the large open areas or trading halls where fairs were held. Then, the merchants set up their displays of cloth, spices, glass, jewelry, or food.

Bells tolled to announce the opening of trading. Cloth markets were held during the first few days of fairs. Merchants bargained with one another and with other customers to get the best prices for their cloth.

▼ *For important deals, merchants signed contracts with one another stating how much of each item they agreed to purchase and for what price. The contracts were signed by the lord's or guild's representative, called a notary, for a fee.*

Food and Spices

When the cloth market closed, a second market began. This market included all kinds of items that had to be weighed, especially food, spices, and dyes. There were raisins, apricots, and oranges from the Middle East. Pepper, ginger, cloves, nutmeg, sugar, cinnamon, and saffron came from India, the Middle East, and the **Far East**. Indigo, a blueish-purple dye, came from India.

◀ *Salt, which needed to be weighed, was sold during the second part of fairs. Salt was used to preserve meat, fish, and butter, to add flavor to food, and to make glass and soap.*

Measuring Goods

Weights and measurements were important when buying and selling goods. Vendors at markets and fairs needed to know how much they were selling so they could calculate what to charge their customers, and buyers needed to make sure they were getting the amount of goods they paid for.

▶ Scales were used by moneychangers to weigh coins, by spice grocers to weigh spices and dyes, and by apothecaries to weigh medicines. Scales measured items in "grains." A "grain" was based on the average weight of a single grain of wheat. Scales measured larger amounts by the ounce, which was about 450 grains, and by the pound, about 7,000 grains.

▲ Farmers measured and sold hay, wheat, and apples by the bushel, half bushel, and quarter bushel, called a peck.

◀ Cloth merchants measured small amounts of fabric in "ells." An ell was about 30 inches (76 centimeters) long. Larger quantities of fabric were measured by the "bolt." A bolt was about 30 ells long.

▼ Wool merchants sold wool by the "sack," which weighed about 364 pounds (165 kilograms).

▶ Vintners and ale makers sold small amounts of wine and ale by the quart and by the gallon. Larger amounts were sold by the barrel, which was equivalent to about 31 gallons (about 141 liters).

Money

In the early Middle Ages, people bought and sold goods by bartering. Bartering means trading one item for another item or exchanging one service for another service. For example, peasants bartered eggs for apples, or bread for fish. Blacksmiths sharpened cobblers' knives, shears, and other tools. In return, cobblers repaired blacksmiths' shoes.

As towns grew and markets became more popular, money replaced bartering. It was easier for people to exchange their goods and services for coins that everyone valued equally.

▲ *The word "bank" comes from the Italian term* banca, *which means "table" or "stall," like the tables and stalls where moneychangers did their trade at shops in towns and at markets and fairs.*

▼ *Moneychangers were the first bankers. They kept records of the coins they exchanged on wax tablets or parchment, which was made from the skin of sheep or goats. They stored the coins in strongboxes with iron locks.*

Coins

Important nobles hired workers called smiths to make coins from metals, such as gold, silver, or copper. Coins differed from one noble's land to another, so moneychangers were needed to exchange one local **currency** for another.

Merchants who traded at European fairs did not want to travel long distances with large bags of coins because they were heavy and could be stolen. Instead, they set up a banking system with moneychangers in which they paid for goods with letters, called fair letters, that stated how much money they owed and when they would pay it.

▶ *Paper money was first used in China in the early 800s. It did not become popular in England until the 1600s, when people who stored their gold and silver in goldsmiths' safes were given written receipts for their goods. People began to use these paper receipts as money.*

Punishing Merchants

Merchants who failed to pay back loans, shaved metal from coins, which made them worth less, cheated on measurements, or sold items of poor quality had their goods taken away. Others were publicly whipped or dragged through the streets. The poor-quality products or false weights were tied around the merchants' necks so that everyone knew why they were being punished. Second-time offenders sometimes had their hands cut off, and third-time offenders were sometimes hanged.

▲ *Moneychangers weighed coins to make sure they were not fake and that they had not been shaved of some of their metal.*

Fun at Fairs

Fairs were centers of fun and entertainment, in addition to being marketplaces. People, from knights to peasants, watched acrobats, jugglers, fire-eaters, and rope walkers. They listened to storytellers and to musicians playing flutes, violins, harps, and drums. They also watched bear-baitings, during which packs of dogs attacked chained bears. This was one of the crueler forms of entertainment during the Middle Ages.

Activities at the Fair

(1) Local brewers, bakers, butchers, fishmongers, winemakers, and farmers set up stalls to sell their goods to hungry and thirsty visitors.

(2) Cordswainers, who made shoes, and potters, who made pitchers and bowls, sold items that people could not make themselves.

(3) Dancing bears, monkeys, and performing horses entertained fair crowds.

(4) Cloth merchants sold fabrics by the bolt to other cloth merchants and to tradespeople who worked with cloth, such as tailors.

The Silk and Spice Routes

The main routes for bringing spices and cloth from the East to fairs in Europe were called the Spice Route and the Silk Road. Merchants bought and sold their goods at trading posts along the way.

The Silk Road

The Silk Road was an overland route that ran for 6,800 miles (11,000 kilometers). It began in China and ended in Constantinople, in Turkey. Chinese merchants carried silk, fine cotton, and other beautiful fabrics on camels over mountains and through deserts. Once they reached Baghdad or Damascus, they traded their goods with Arab merchants. The Arab merchants then took the goods overland or by ship to Constantinople. From there, merchants from Venice shipped the fabrics to Italy.

▲ *Italian merchant ships brought goods from Arab ports to ports in Italy, including Venice. By the 1160s, Venice had become one of the richest ports in Europe. Its harbor was filled with docks, warehouses, and shipbuilding and repair facilities.*

The Spice Route

The Spice Route was the sea and land route through which spices were brought from China, India, the Middle East, and the Spice Islands. The Spice Islands, which are now known as Indonesia, were named for the valuable spices grown there. Spices were very popular with wealthy medieval Europeans, who used them to flavor their food and to make perfumes and medicines.

Most of the Spice Route was traveled by merchants from China, India, and the Middle East. They transported their goods by boat and by horse or camel caravans. Italian merchants picked up the spices at ports along the Mediterranean Sea and shipped them to Italy. From there, the spices were taken to markets and fairs throughout Europe.

▲ *Arab merchants weighed spices to determine their prices before selling them. Many spices were used to make perfumes.*

▼ *The two main trading routes from Asia to Europe were the Silk Road, which went over land, shown here by the dotted line, and the Spice Route, which went by sea, shown here by the solid line.*

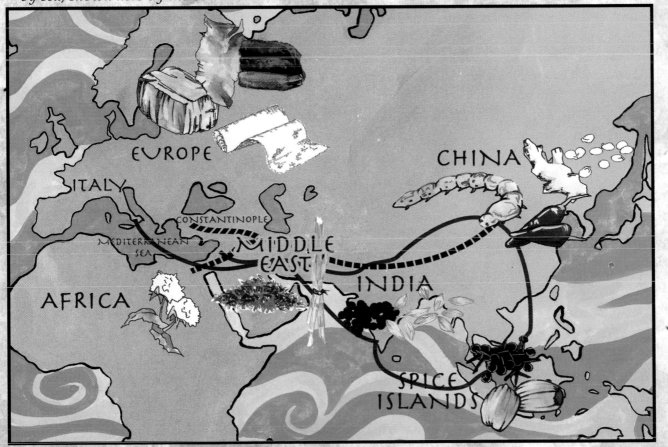

EUROPE

ITALY

CHINA

CONSTANTINOPLE

MEDITERRANEAN SEA

MIDDLE EAST

INDIA

AFRICA

SPICE ISLANDS

25

Other Travelers

Most people in the Middle Ages did not travel far from home, but there were a few groups, besides merchants, who journeyed long distances.

Nobles

Nobles traveled for work and for pleasure. They visited their lands to make sure their manors were being managed properly. They traveled to important events, such as the coronation, or crowning, of a king, the **dubbing** of a knight, or the marriage of a family member. They also traveled to wage war on other nobles trying to take over their land, to go on crusade, and to take part in **tournaments**.

Nobles journeyed in large parties of 30 to 60 people. They were accompanied by their families, soldiers, officials, priests, doctors, and servants.

It was the responsibility of servants, called herbergers, to find a place for the traveling party to stay at night. Usually, everyone stayed for free at other nobles' castles or in monasteries. These places did not look forward to the visits. It was often very expensive to feed and house a noble's entire traveling party, which sometimes stayed for days or weeks. If nobles had nowhere else to stay, they paid to stay at inns.

◀ *Nobles traveled on horseback or in carriages pulled by horses. Servants walked beside horse-drawn wagons filled with food, clothing, and furniture.*

Crusaders

From 1096 to 1291, knights and other Christians traveled to the Holy Land to fight a series of wars, called the crusades. They wanted to recapture the area from **Muslims** who ruled it at the time. The journey to the Holy Land was long and difficult. Many people died along the way from hunger, thirst, and illness.

▶ *Some crusaders who arrived in the Holy Land were not prepared to fight in the hot, dry climate and died during battle.*

Pilgrims

Pilgrims are people who travel to saints' shrines and other places of religious importance. In the Middle Ages, most people traveled to pilgrimage sites near their homes, but more adventurous Christian pilgrims traveled to Rome, in Italy, where **relics** of various saints were housed; Santiago de Compostela, in northern Spain, where Saint James was buried; Canterbury Cathedral, in England, where the **archbishop** Thomas Becket was buried; and the Holy Land, where Jesus Christ, who Christians believe is the son of God, lived.

Christians were not the only medieval pilgrims. Muslims were required to visit the *Ka'bah*, a holy shrine in Mecca, in present-day Saudi Arabia, at least once in their lifetime. Hundreds of thousands of Muslims flocked to Mecca during the Middle Ages.

◀ *Pilgrims who visited holy places usually bought souvenirs, such as flasks of holy water, miniature statues of saints, and badges with pictures of the saint carved on them. The symbol for the pilgrims of Santiago de Compostela was a shell.*

Transportation

People in the Middle Ages had two options when traveling: to go by land or by water. When traveling by land, most people walked, even if they were going very long distances. Nobles and wealthier people rode on horseback or donkey. Goods were transported by pack animals, carts, or carriages pulled by horses or oxen.

▲ People paid local lords to use their roads and bridges. Most roads were made of dirt and were very narrow. When it rained, they were muddy and filled with potholes. When it was hot and dry, they were very dusty.

Finding the Way

Signposts were not common on medieval roads since most people could not read. Travelers relied on their memories or they hired local guides, who were usually shepherds, to lead them to their destinations. Travelers in the Alps, a mountain range in western Europe, sometimes placed small pyramids of rocks beside roads to mark the main travel routes. There were some maps and travel guides, especially for pilgrims. The guides included information on inns and **taverns** where pilgrims could rest during their journeys.

Medieval Highway Rules

In Europe, most roads in the Middle Ages were only wide enough for one cart, so travelers had to obey certain rules of the road. Larger, heavier vehicles had the right of way. An empty cart yielded to a full cart, and a small cart gave way to a large cart. If a person traveling by cart met a person on horseback, the horseback rider stepped aside for the cart. If the horseback rider met a pedestrian, the pedestrian let the horseback rider pass.

Roads Around the World

Roads in other parts of the world were more advanced than those in Europe. The Inca Empire, in South America, built a sophisticated system of roads that linked all parts of their **empire** with their capital city, Cuzco. The main roads were paved with huge flat stones, and suspension bridges hung over ravines and rivers. Shelters for travelers were also built along the roads.

Traveling by Water

People in the Middle Ages also used rivers and canals to get from place to place. Large ships sailed along major rivers, such as the Seine, in France. Smaller boats traveled along narrower, more shallow rivers.

▼ Small ferries driven by ferrymen, who used poles and oars to move the boats, carried passengers and their baggage along small, shallow rivers and streams. Nobles entered the city gates by horseback.

Explorers

Many people in the Middle Ages were curious about the world around them, but travel was so dangerous that they needed good reasons to explore far-away lands. Some explorers searched for more land, others wanted to find riches or new trade routes, and still others wanted to convert people to their religion.

◀ Leif Eriksson

The **Viking** adventurer Leif Eriksson was one of the first Europeans to reach the coast of North America, around 1000 A.D. He traveled to the area in a Viking cargo ship, called a *knarr*, and landed on the eastern coast of present-day Canada. Eriksson named the area Vinland because of the wild vines that grew there.

Marco Polo ▶

Marco Polo was an Italian merchant who explored China beginning in 1271. Polo was trying to find a way to trade directly with the Chinese, instead of dealing with Arab merchants. His book, *The Adventures of Marco Polo*, describes the long journey, the customs of the Chinese, and the court of the Mongol leader, Kublai Khan.

Ibn Battuta

Ibn Battuta was a Moroccan adventurer who traveled in the 1300s. In his 30 years and more than 75,000 miles (120,000 kilometers) of travel, he journeyed through Africa, Asia, India, the Middle East, and parts of Europe. He described his land and sea travels, his attack by thieves, and his near-drowning in a sinking ship in the book *The Travels of Ibn Battuta*.

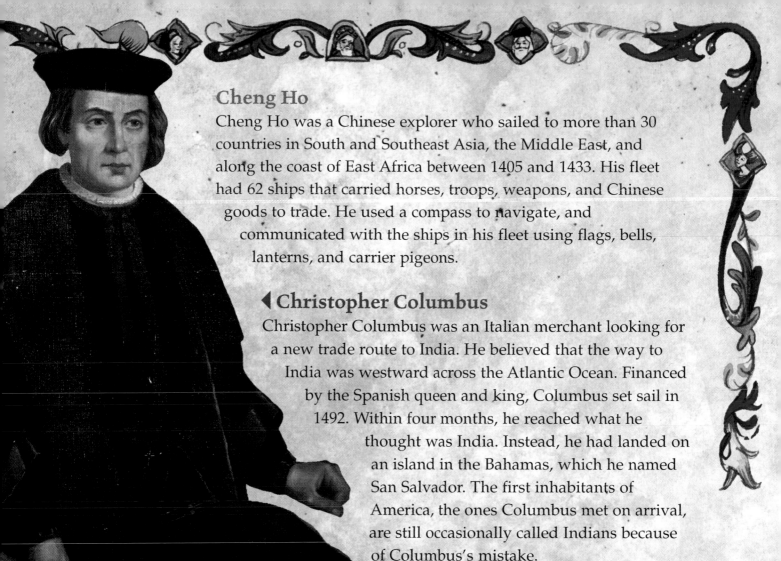

Cheng Ho

Cheng Ho was a Chinese explorer who sailed to more than 30 countries in South and Southeast Asia, the Middle East, and along the coast of East Africa between 1405 and 1433. His fleet had 62 ships that carried horses, troops, weapons, and Chinese goods to trade. He used a compass to navigate, and communicated with the ships in his fleet using flags, bells, lanterns, and carrier pigeons.

◄ Christopher Columbus

Christopher Columbus was an Italian merchant looking for a new trade route to India. He believed that the way to India was westward across the Atlantic Ocean. Financed by the Spanish queen and king, Columbus set sail in 1492. Within four months, he reached what he thought was India. Instead, he had landed on an island in the Bahamas, which he named San Salvador. The first inhabitants of America, the ones Columbus met on arrival, are still occasionally called Indians because of Columbus's mistake.

Explorers' Tools

Certain inventions helped medieval explorers. Triangle sails invented by Arab sailors in the 1100s made sailing in light winds easier, and stronger ship designs enabled explorers to travel in rougher waters. The magnetic compass helped explorers tell direction, and the astrolabe helped them read **latitude**. More accurate maps and increased knowledge about wind direction and ocean currents also helped explorers.

▶ *Astrolabes, which were invented by Muslims, were used to measure the angles of stars above the horizon. With that information, navigators could determine their ships' positions on the ocean.*

Glossary

archbishop An important Christian religious leader who is responsible for a large area known as an archdiocese

archer A soldier trained to use a bow and arrow

astronomy The study of the stars and planets

chamber pot A bowl used in the home as a toilet

Christian Belonging to the religion of Christianity, which follows the teachings of God and his son on earth, Jesus Christ

cobbler A person who mends or makes boots and shoes

currency Money

dubbing The act of giving a person the title of knighthood

empire A group of countries or territories under one ruler or government

Far East Eastern and southeastern Asia, especially the countries of China, Japan, North Korea, South Korea, and Mongolia

Flemish From Flanders, a Dutch-speaking region in northern Belgium

Holy Land An area in present-day Israel, Jordan, and Syria that has special religious meaning for Christians, Muslims, and Jews

Islam A religion based on the teachings of God, whom Muslims call Allah, and his prophets

latitude The distance, measured in degrees, north or south of the equator. The equator is an imaginary line through the center of the earth.

mason A person who builds with stone or brick

merchant A person who buys and sells goods

Middle East A region made up of southwestern Asia and northern Africa

mortarer A worker who mixes mortar, which is a blend of sand, lime, water, and sometimes cement, to hold bricks and stones together

Muslim A person who believes in Islam

pilgrim A person who makes a religious journey to a sacred place

port A place where ships load and unload cargo

relic Something that belonged to a holy person, such as clothing or a body part

shrine A small area or structure dedicated to a god or saint

tavern A place that sells food and drinks

tax Payment in the form of money, services, crops, or livestock

thatch Straw woven together to make a roof

toll A fee charged to enter a town, cross a bridge, or travel along a road

tournament A sporting contest between knights on horseback

Viking A member of a Scandinavian people who raided the coasts of Europe from the 700s to 900s

Index

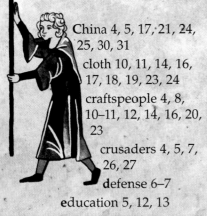
1 2 3 4 5 6 7 8 9 0   Printed in the U.S.A.   0 9 8 7 6 5 4